A TALE OF THREE BOATS

D1502527

A TALE OF
THREE
BOATS

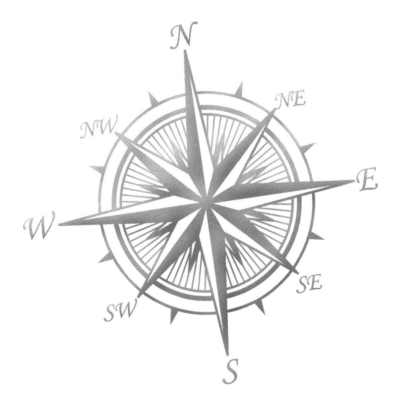

Robert Higgins
OLD SAYBROOK, CT

Cover & Book Design by Words by Jen (Branford, CT)
Printed in the U.S.A.

ISBN: 978-0-578-42755-3

*This book is for my wife Suzanne
and my daughters Christine and Katharyn.*

Foreword

THE FOLLOWING THREE ACCOUNTINGS ARE a sort-of rambling reminiscence of an octogenarian who has always loved boats and most anything to do with the sea. The first, "The Story of Devnet," deals with the restoration of a derelict yacht, which I had stumbled upon and demonstrates what a naive soul I was to think I was up to job, but somehow I was!

The second story, "The Flight of the Phoenix," is partly about a sting operation and the careful planning that went into it. Again, my naivete can be seen in my readily accepting the word of a man who turned out to be a perfect scoundrel. The plot took on a certain Hollywood-esque theme and provided those involved with it a degree of adventure and excitement.

The final story, "A Cruising Log Of Eidolon," is from the log of a wonderful cruise that my wife and I took on our own boat, from Connecticut to Florida and back. For us it truly was a dream come true. We took six months to slowly travel the Intracoastal Waterway (ICW), and passages outside, to visit many spots we had missed on previous trips.

My brother, Richard, published his memoir several years ago, and it was very well done indeed. When I read it, I was impressed with what he had accomplished in his lifetime. The following is not intended as a memoir since it only depicts three relatively recent periods of my life. And while my brother's achievements were largely academic, my achievements, if I may call them such, were of a more physical nature. I always enjoyed working with my hands, and producing things that could be seen, and touched, rather than conceptual ideas. As you'll read, my interests centered largely around boats and sailing. The three stories told here are but a small part of my lifelong adventures in, around, and on the water.

Perhaps I have not mentioned my wife, Suzanne, enough in these writings. If so, that is merely oversight on my part, for she plays very prominently in all three of the stories, as well as all other aspects of my life.

"There is nothing-absolutely nothing-half so much worth doing as simply messing about in boats." — Ratty

THE STORY OF DEVNET

1978 through 1990

1978 – Danbury, Connecticut

AS VIEWED FROM THE HIGHWAY (I-84) the old sailboat looked very forlorn. It sat in a clumsy wooden cradle alongside an industrial looking building. The forward most section of the bow was missing as was most of the planking below the waterline. It had the appearance of having been in this state for a very long time. As beat up as she looked, I could see that her original lines had been graceful, and viewed from afar they seemed to have held their shape. She appeared to be about 40 feet in length.

At this time I was running my small home improvement company and as luck would have it, the rather industrial building next to the boat turned out to be a cabinet making concern whose services I had occasion to need. So I called on them and met the owner, one Albert Ackel. As we discussed a certain countertop I needed for my business, I casually asked Mr. Ackel what the backstory of the boat was. Well, old Albert's eyes lit up and he asked me if I would like to buy it!

"No way," I replied, "I'm just curious about what a sailboat this big is doing so far from the saltwater." So Albert proceeded to tell me why she happened to be there.

"About three years ago, a man came to see me with a request to restore a boat he had bought. He explained that a former owner had radically modified the boat with the idea of doing some serious racing. He had the engine removed to reduce weight, added an over long mast for more sail area, made changes to the cockpit for streamlining. Below deck the galley was removed and bunks and bulkheads were removed. The wooden hull was then covered with a layer of fiberglass cloth."

These changes had been made some time ago, and before they were finished, they were abandoned and the boat quickly deteriorated, until the new owner bought her and approached Ackel to restore the boat to its original shape. The owner told Ackel that the boat had some history. [1]

....

1 The owner told Ackel that the boat, whose name was CHRISTINA, was listed in Lloyd's Registry of American Yachts. I researched CHRISTINA, and found she was formerly FALCON, and was built in Holland by Amsterdamer Scheeps in 1951 to a Devries Lentch design. Her principal dimensions were shown as 38 feet overall, by 10 ½ feet beam and 6 feet of draught. Her rig was described as that of a yawl, and in the process of removing the fiberglass covering in the aft sections, it was evident that there had been chainplates for the rigging of a mizzen mast.

Ackel agreed to do the job. So the owner hired a rigging/moving company to move the boat, in its cradle, to just outside Ackel's shop. Although he was an accomplished cabinet maker, Ackel knew little about wooden boat construction and soon found himself over his head with the project. He started by removing all the fir ceiling planking, which, without bulkheads went all the way from stem to stern.

Then, without further ado, the owner disappeared and abandoned the project! It seems he had left his wife and run off to Europe with his secretary, leaving Ackel holding the bag.

After some time had gone by with no sign of the owner returning, Ackel took steps to obtain legal ownership of the boat with the idea of selling it, probably to some sucker like me.

It occurred to me that maybe this was a viable project so I asked Ackel what he would take for the boat. He replied that he would sell it for what labor he had invested in it, around $1000. I took the bait and gave him a check for the deal. All that remained for me was to have it moved to my home, next to my barn, which was my workshop. A rigging/moving company agreed to do the job for $500 and a few days later she was installed next to the barn. This turned out to be an excellent position. It seemed that the deck level of the boat was even with the second story of

Work begins on DEVNET, 1978

the barn, which was where my workshop was. A sliding door in the barn, previously used for loading hay, opened directly to the cockpit area of the boat. Ideal for working aboard without going up and down a ladder.

I was pretty new at this kind of work myself. What was needed at first was to replace metal frames that had largely rusted away. Every third frame was fashioned from galvanized angle iron and the galvanization had mostly disappeared in the bilge areas. Where the rusted frames met the planking, they rotted the wood, which explained why most of the planking below the water line was gone. The wooden frames between the metal ones were in pretty bad shape as well and needed replacing. What amazed me was the fact that the boat was in no way "hogged" and had maintained her original lines.

Before I started work in earnest, I needed to get rid of the bulky cradle she sat in since it was very awkward working around it. So I bought six #1 sailboat jack stands from Brownell and carefully arranged them two at a time while I demolished the old cradle.

I started to fashion replacement frames by laminating ¼ inch strips of white oak using Resorcinol glue. This went rather quickly, and I soon

Fiberglass applied to port side

had most the frames ready for planking. I found a source of boat lumber in White Plains, NY at Condon Lumber and bought a bunch of Philippine mahogany for planking.

After installing both garboards, I decided that, what with working eight hours a days at the home improvement job, I didn't really have the energy to work on the boat in the evenings, so I declared an hiatus, and I didn't know for how long.

Fast Forward Seven Years - 1985

ONE COLD AND RAINY DAY in early March my wife, Suzanne, and I entertained a couple for the weekend. We were friendly with the lady but had not met her beau before this. After introductions Jim, the boyfriend, asked about the sailboat next to the barn. I explained the situation, and the fact that I had stopped work on it years before.

"Let me have a look at it," Jim said, and so I took him out to the barn where we went upstairs, and over to the boat. It was lightly raining so we went below for shelter. The below space was one big open area with no

Deck installed, house lowered to deck

bulkheads, or anything else for that matter. Green mold, if not moss, was evident all over and she really looked forlorn and abandoned.

"WOW," Jim declared. "She looks beautiful! Why did you stop work on her?" I replied that I was tired of pounding nails all day, and then coming to work on her in the evenings and weekends.

"You've got a great potential here, you should get back to work on her," Jim said, and as he did I realized how right he was, I had to at least try to finish the job. In my childhood I had read a story about a boat and a small dog, both of which were named DEVNET. I liked the name, which meant white wave, and decided that was going to be my new boat's name. So work began in earnest.

The new frames were in place from my previous attempts at restoration, also the new garboards were installed. So now I attacked the rest of the planking, with many trips back and forth to Condon Lumber in White Plains, mostly for Philippine mahogany.

Before starting the planking, I designed and had fabricated, new stainless steel floor timbers. Each was bolted to a pair of frames, and had holes for keel bolts. I had discovered early on that the original keel bolts, which were silicon bronze, had de-zincafied and were as brittle as toast.

DEVNET nearly finished

Installing new keel bolts was quite a job. I used ¾ inch SS threaded rod, and drilled holes through the floors, the keelson, and through as much as 18 inches of the lead ballast keel. I couldn't find an auger bit long enough for the job, so I welded an extension to the longest bit I could find. This worked fine except that, when drilling, I had to pull the bit out before the drilling spoils reached the top end of the bit flutes and clean them out. If I didn't pull out soon enough, the spoils would jam around the beginning of the welded extension causing a monstrous jam up. It took a come-along rigged up to extract the bit on these occasions!

When all the keel bolt holes had been drilled, I needed a way to countersink the bottom ends to receive the nuts on the threaded rod. To do this I drove ¾ inch tapered dowels into the holes so that I could center a one and 1-½ inch Forstner bit to do the countersinking. Working under the keel was not a lot of fun!

The rudder was not in very good condition. It was fashioned of white oak with a rudder post made of 1-½ inch solid stainless steel which started at the very bottom of the rudder, up and around the propeller aperture, and on up through the deck. Since there had been no cockpit, the rudder post was made long enough to project through the deck, making it very long. By digging a very deep hole, I was able to

DEVNET sailing in a brisk breeze, wife Sue at the helm

drop the rudder. What with the heavy oak, and all the stainless steel, the rudder altogether weighed a whopping two hundred and fifty pounds! That needed attention.

To make a new rudder, I first had fabricated a new post of 1 ½ inch stainless tubing, with four "fingers" projecting aft. Next, I fashioned the new control surface out of several layers of ½ inch Airex foam glued up with epoxy. The finished product weighed only forty pounds, a saving of two hundred and ten pounds!

The planking was going smoothly, but I soon realized that I was not good enough at boat carpentry to make good, caulkable seams. It's an art!

At about this time I came upon a book by Allan Vaitses called *Covering Wooden Boats With Fiberglass*. This book made the whole project doable. Without it, I would have abandoned the job. Now irregular spaces between planks became an asset rather than a liability. Alan advises the two factors that make this process viable are one: mechanically fastening the glass to the wooden hull and two: using enough layers of glass, of various types, to make significant thickness.

Before starting the glassing process, I had to prepare the hull by removing any vestiges of fiberglass material that had been previously applied. This was easy because it had failed for the most part, and it just needed to be peeled off. Next a thorough sanding of the whole hull using very coarse sandpaper for better adhesion of the first layer of glass.

Next, taking a tip from Alan, I had to tip the hull about 15 - 20 degrees so that I wasn't working directly overhead when laying on the glass. Tipping the hull was a little scary, but it went okay by gradually slacking off the jack stands on one side and tightening up on the other. Once all the weight of the lean was on one side it was just a matter of gradually slacking off that side, one stand at a time, going from bow to stern.

I should mention that the keel was sitting on several railroad ties running athwartships. To prevent the keel from kicking out, I secured another tie fore and aft up alongside the keel. (Of course this whole process would need to be repeated later on the other side.) Starting with a layer of 4 oz. matt, I wet down the hull and applied the sheets vertically, then I thoroughly wet down the matt. Because the hull was tilted, the job was much easier than had it been upright.

The resin I was using was epoxy purchased from Defender Industries in 5 gallon pails. At the end of the glassing, I totaled up the epoxy as 21 five gallon pails, for a total of 105 gallons!

After several vertical sheets of matt were applied, before the first sheets were getting too hard, I drove ¾ inch galvanized roofing nails into the hull through the matt, with spacing about 4 inches in each direction. This was the mechanical fastening that Alan had recommended.

After the entire side of the hull was covered with matt, and secured with roofing nails, I applied a layer of heavy woven roving and then another layer of 4 oz. matt. The total thickness was now over ¼ inch, enough to satisfy Allan's recommendation. Together with the thickness of the glass, and the mechanical fastening, the result was a solid fiber-glass enclosure that should last for years. Note: 25 years later, the hull remained in excellent condition.

Next, after leaning the hull in the opposite direction, and repeating the fiberglass application, it was time to address the house and the deck. The deck was teak, laid sprung, and was in very bad shape, with multiple holes for various deck hardware, and some missing pieces, so I decided to remove it and replace with marine plywood. To make this job easier, I decided to lift the house off the deck and prop it up out of the way.

I should mention here that the previous owners had decked over what had been the cockpit as part of the plan to streamline the boat for racing.

Before installing the plywood decking, I had to reframe the cockpit, putting in the sole and sides. That done, I put down the plywood, and fiber-glassed it, including the inside of the cockpit. After that, I lowered the house back down to the deck and fiber-glassed it entirely.

The next step involved creating the bulwarks on the deck. From about six inches high at the bow, they were four inches high further aft. The material was Philippine mahogany and was fastened to the deck with eight and six inch drifts. Once installed, the bulwarks were fiber-glassed on the inside and outside. The outside was faired into the existing fiberglass on the topsides. Eventually the bulwarks would have teak cap rails installed.

Now came the job of finishing the below deck areas. First off was to lay down a subfloor for the cabin sole, so as to have something to walk on when working below. Next, I positioned and installed bulkheads, either side of the galley, and forward of the saloon. Then I built two pilot berths, and two more bunks in the saloon. Then I installed ceiling planking of white ash throughout, while all the time running electrical wiring and plumbing.

The next big, big job was powering. I was able to buy a power package from VETUS MARINE which included a 3 cylinder, 22 HP diesel, engine controls, panel, water lift, muffler, exhaust hose, two 12 volt batteries and the proper sized propeller. The only thing not included was a shaft, for obvious reasons. The whole package cost only $2500!

I constructed the engine bed by fastening two six foot lengths of ¼ inch by two inch steel flat stock onto four frames and fit two inch oak beds on top of the steel. With a lot of sweating and swearing, I managed to squeeze the engine onto the beds, going through the opening to the engine space behind the companionway ladder. Believe it or not, everything fit nicely. HOWEVER, once in place, there was no way to secure the after engine mounts to the bed. I couldn't get at them from the companionway hatch area. Furthermore, I realized that there would be no access to such areas as the oil pump, and dipstick for changing the lube oil. SOLUTION, cut a hatch opening in the cockpit sole. This gave easy access to all areas previously unreachable.

The mast that had come with the boat, had been stored on the ground in a field nearby, and since it was wooden, it was thoroughly rotted. Be-

DEVNET at Island Cove Marina

sides that, it was much too tall for the boat as it was intended to be part of the racing scene. So, where to find a suitable replacement?

The answer, an ad in one of the boating magazines for a metal mast off a C&C 34 that was for sale by the owner who had installed a new bendy rig on his boat. The mast was in Michigan but I was able to get a transporter to piggyback it on a boat delivery coming east. Didn't cost too much for the mast and the shipping.

When the mast arrived, I had a friend who owned a crane, step the mast for a fit. (The mast came with all the standing rigging, which was rod rigging!) Because of the high aspect rig on the shorter C&C, the headstay and backstay were too short, but the shrouds were too long. After taking all the necessary measurements, we pulled the mast out and I took the rigging off and brought it all to Chuck Poindexter at Sound Rigging in Essex, CT.

Chuck shortened the upper and lower shrouds about six inches each. He then fashioned a three foot extension for the backstay, and made up a new headstay, since I couldn't add to the existing one.

Now a lot of painting and varnishing took place, and suddenly, it was time to arrange for transporting to salt water. But first, it was necessary to move the boat from where it was located beside the barn, to the front of the barn. This was accomplished using the same crane that put the boat beside the barn eight years earlier. I took some pictures of this process, one showing the boat in slings high over the barn. It occurred to me at this point that if anything let go, I would have lost the boat, and the barn, and my truck that was in the barn! Luckily, all went smoothly.

Next, I hired a yacht transporter to move the boat to Chimney Point Marina in Old Saybrook, CT.

Once the boat was loaded onto the Brownell Trailer that the transporter was using, and the mast secured alongside, we set out for Old Saybrook. Suzanne and I followed the transporter in our car, and our neighbor and friend Joe Baker, with his sister Paula, followed us in their car. Joe was a cameraman for ESPN and with a borrowed camera, filmed the entire trip to Old Saybrook! (Later, he borrowed our photo album of all the pics we had taken of the project and made up a wonderful video, starting with the very first pictures of what seemed to be a wreck, to shots of us sailing the finished product, all captioned and scored!

When we arrived at Chimney Point Marina, we had a minor disappointment. By previous arrangement, we had expected to be taken di-

Bob and Sue for a sail on DEVNET

rectly off the transporter, and launched. However, the yard manager told us that the travel lift was occupied, and we couldn't launch until the next day. Sue was annoyed and told the manger so, in no uncertain terms, but I was secretly relieved. I had already had enough excitement for one day, and I was very nervous about how the boat would sit in the water. I had made an educated guess as to where the waterline should be. I could wait until the morning to see how good my guess was.

The next morning we splashed, and to my relief, my waterline guess proved to be good! We moved over to the rigging dock, stepped the mast, which had been outfitted with wiring and running rigging, and tuned the rig. Then we moved to our slip. Lots of excitement!

We had earlier ordered sails, per my measurements, from a loft in Maine, and I had bought a new metal boom. It was lots of fun bending on the sails, running sheets, etc. Everything fit according to plan.

I had earlier installed halyard winches on deck, and large Lewmar sheet winches in the cockpit, so now with everything ready to go, it only remained to take her out for a sail.

Our first sail on DEVNET was the beginning of a wonderful relationship with a truly great boat. She sailed like a dream, went to wind handily, screamed on a beam reach, and did remarkably well in light air.

At about this time a fellow from a nearby neighborhood of ours, an old Florida Cracker named Wade, stopped by our house and said to me "Bob, I have to apologize to you." I asked him what on earth for. "Because when I saw that wreck of a boat sitting next to your barn all those years, I said to myself, and anybody who would listen, that boat will NEVER see the water again! Well, by God you did it! Congratulations."

After an abbreviated first season, August through October, mostly day sailing, we came to know a lot about her, and were anxious to do some cruising the following summer.

Summer of 1988 saw us cruising all around eastern Long Island Sound and Narragansett Bay. In succeeding summers, we extended our cruising grounds to include Block Island, the Vineyard, the Elizabeth Islands, Cape Cod and Nantucket. In all, we enjoyed DEVNET for about five years, up until we fell in love with EIDOLON. But that's another story for another time.

THE FLIGHT OF THE PHOENIX

April 1990 through May 1994

4/15/90 Old Saybrook, CT
Offshore East Marina

ONE EARLY SPRING MORNING, I noticed a peculiar vessel in the marina's mooring field. She was a schooner of some size, 60 or 70 feet in length. I borrowed the marina's work boat and headed out to inspect. The schooner was painted white and appeared to be of steel construction, rust was present and the overall condition was decidedly run down. I circled her twice and was fascinated. She had a clipper bow and a long bowsprit, and what appeared to be a large cargo hatch cover midships, an on deck steering station, and a pilot house and <u>raised</u> deckhouse aft. Both the main and foremasts were without topmasts and appeared somewhat stubby, but on the whole the vessel looked to be a sturdy, honest workboat type.

After my initial inspection, I was anxious to learn more about this strange boat so I headed back to the marina and sought out Art Galotti, one of the marina's operators. Art informed me that the schooner, PHOENIX, belonged to a young man by the name of Gil Johnson who had just recently come to the marina, and was looking for a place to refurbish her for work in the charter trade. Art also told me that Gil was looking for a partner who could invest in the project, and suggested that I get together with him for a talk.

Two days later I met with Johnson and got a run down on the situation. It seems that he did not own PHOENIX, but had entered into a purchase agreement with the actual owner, one Greg Brazier of Glen Cove Long Island.

Johnson's plan was to bring the boat up to par for passing a Coast Guard inspection to allow for carrying paying passengers as an excursion/charter boat. He had made an initial payment to Brazier, but currently had no funds for improvements. That's where I could be of service as partner and investor.

With very little formality, we did enter into a partnership agreement and with my funds, we began work on shaping PHOENIX up for service and Coast Guard inspection. Thus began two months of frantic work. With cutting torch and sand blasting, carpentry and painting she was starting to look pretty fair. By the time we got the Coast Guard involved we were well on our way.

PHOENIX at home on the Connecticut River

Note: With the partnership agreement, I was to make monthly mortgage payments (which were already in arrears) and make monthly insurance premium payments, as well as supplying needed working capital against Gil's contribution of the vessel itself.

Coast Guard certification was largely possible because she had been previously certified for 49 day passengers, although that certificate had expired. The recertify process was nevertheless somewhat daunting, but we finally made it through, and now we were ready to start carrying paying passengers. By now it was almost August and the season was more than half over. We were able to negotiate a deal that allowed us to sail from the Dock and Dine Restaurant in Old Saybrook for two hour cruises. And so it began.

Almost immediately two problems became apparent. First, while we were entitled to use Dock and Dine's dock, we did not have exclusive rights. Other Dock and Dine customers could also use the dock. On more than one occasion, when we returned from a cruise, there was no room at the dock to unload passengers! Some scrambling was necessary on those occasions. The second problem that became apparent was the lack of traffic for paying customers. There was traffic of a sort, sometimes busloads of Elderhostel folks, but they were not inclined to take sightseeing cruises with us. Other traffic was sporadic at best and yielded little revenue.

These two problems called for a new plan and a new venue for our project. Enter the Connecticut River Museum, and their Steamboat Dock. The museum was very receptive to our approach and welcomed our presence at their dock. We did not need to pay for running our business there as the museum saw us as a draw for their other exhibits.

From when we first started to sail from Steamboat Dock, business was brisk. We launched some successful advertising and all was looking up. We started to get some corporate charters and formed some plans for winter projects on the boat and for next season.

Over the first winter we made some physical improvements. Four new bunks in the focsil, and upgrades in the galley.

The second season was profitable, and we started getting a lot of repeat business, as well as even more corporate charter work. When the second season was drawing to a close we made some plans for the coming winter.

Gil felt that in order to make a go of the whole project, we should operate during the winter in the Bahamas. I met this idea with mixed feelings. While I thought it would be great to have the boat at work during the winter, I was not about to leave my family at home while I played down south. So we came to this agreement.

Gil would take the boat to the Bahamas and would operate out of Port Lucaya. He would assume all monthly payments (which I had been making) and any revenue he could generate would accrue to him.

Off went PHOENIX to Port Lucaya!

At this point I had my first inkling that Gil was not exactly on the up and up. After PHOENIX left, I discovered that he had removed the LORAN-C receiver from my own boat and taken it without my permission.

Gil and I maintained phone contact and aside from some minor mechanical problems, the trip south seemed to be going relatively smoothly. When PHOENIX arrived in Port Lucaya, Gil phoned and told me he had established contact with a water concession and would be taking on paying passengers soon.

He had hired a local captain (Gil did not hold a license himself.)

Several weeks passed and nothing new.

Then all hell broke loose!

Greg Brazier called me and informed me that he had not received the past several monthly mortgage payments, and that our insurance company had lapsed our coverage for lack of premium payment, both payments that I had been making, but now Gil was to be making.

At this time I informed Greg that Gil was now responsible for the payments as he had taken PHOENIX to the Bahamas for the winter season and was running the boat there.

Greg was shocked at this news!

Note: I had never seen whatever purchase agreement that Gil had with Greg. Gil claimed that he did not have a copy to show me. He simply told me what it contained, and I foolishly believed him.

Now Greg told me that according to the purchase agreement, he had the right to repossess PHOENIX for any one of three reasons:

1.   Non payment of the monthly mortgage.
2.   Lapse of insurance coverage.
3.   Taking the boat out of U.S. waters.

By now Gil had stopped answering my phone calls after repeated attempts to reach him. At about this time, a former deckhand we had employed called me and said that he was going on vacation in Port Lucaya and would locate PHOENIX and call me with any news.

A week later, Bob, the former deckhand, called from Port Lucaya and told me that Gil had signed a contract to charter her to the water sports concession and apparently had no intention of bringing PHOENIX back to Connecticut in the spring. That was a blow, but not entirely unexpected since Gil had by this time cut off all communications with me. I finally realized what a scoundrel he was. I called Greg and told him the news.

Several weeks went by before I heard back from Greg. "Bob, I have a plan to get PHOENIX back. Would you be willing to participate in the plan?" he asked.

"What's the plan"? I asked.

"I can't tell you at this time, but I have to know if you're on board," he replied.

I was worried that he might get me involved in something illegal, so I hesitated.

"I promise you that there will be no laws broken, but I cannot tell you any more at this time because absolute secrecy is necessary!"

Still, I would not commit without knowing more.

A week went by, then Greg called and agreed to tell all, so the scam was revealed to me.

"My father is a retired actor," Greg said. "He and I have set up a phony company that claims to produce MTV videos for the television industry. We will call the company *Global Site Locators, serving the film industry since 1981* and print appropriate business cards and contract forms."

"The plan calls for my father to fly to Port Lucaya, find PHOENIX and approach Gil with a proposition." Greg was very concerned that somehow, Gil might get word of the plan, so I was sworn to secrecy.

The Proposition as it was made to Gil:

"We would like to use PHOENIX in the production of an MTV video. We will pay five thousand dollars a day for the use of the boat. Expect the shoot to take at least five days. We will include you and your crew in the video, and we'll put you and your crew up in a first class hotel in Boca Raton for the duration of the shoot."

Gil said that he would consider the offer and was left with a business card including a phone number in Laguna Beach California. The phone actually belonged to Greg's sister who lived there. Gil was aware that he had taken the boat out of the country in violation of the purchase agreement, so he was naturally suspicious of this whole approach.

Note: Gil was told that in order for the plan to go forward, the shoot had to take place in Fort Lauderdale, FL. because Greg's attorney had warned us that repossessing the boat in the Bahamas could be a problem. We had to get the boat into U.S. waters. Furthermore, Gil was instructed to have an all white crew on board as we did not want to be responsible for returning native Bahamians to the Islands.

As Gil pondered the situation, he called the number in Laguna Beach. Greg's sister had agreed to answer any incoming calls, for a period of time, with the greeting "Hello, *Global Site Locators*" and did so when Gil called. He questioned the veracity of the proposal and was assured that it was on the level. Further, he was told that the boat was to be at the Best Western Marina in Fort Lauderdale no later than 5 P.M. on the following Friday. After docking, he and his crew would be picked up by a limo and delivered to hotel X in Boca Raton.

Meanwhile, back in Connecticut, I was to assemble a repo crew and swear them to secrecy. I selected Art Galotti and Rodney Weimer for the job. Unfortunately, one of the crew members, when at our local watering hole, let slip what was going on and I had a request from another local to join the party. I strongly denied that any such event was happening, and was able to quash the rumor before it spread. That was a close call, because Gil had contacts who frequented that watering hole.

On the day before PHOENIX was due in Florida, Greg, Art, Rodney and I flew to Lauderdale. Greg was along to coordinate the effort, but would not be coming back with the boat. That evening we all checked into a motel, had a nice dinner, and went to bed. In the morning, we went shopping for supplies and groceries for the trip and filled several jerry cans with diesel, in case we needed that for a quick getaway.

The plan was for PHOENIX to be met at the Best Western Marina with a limo to take the crew to a first class hotel in Boca Raton. At this point we did not know if Gil had taken the bait, or if he had somehow figured out the scam.

Later in the morning, we decided to scope out the marina. While we were crossing the 17th Street bridge in our rented van we could see PHOENIX just pulling into a slip at the marina, well ahead of schedule. Whew! They had bought it!

Now, before the 5PM limo pick up, we decided to surveil the situation and determine just who was aboard. Again, we did not want the complications of a native crew. Equipped with binoculars we performed a stake out!

Somehow Rodney found a way to get to the roof of the Best Western, and I found a spot on the opposite bank of the ICW in a grove of trees. We each had handheld VHF radios for our communications. After two hours we had identified all onboard. Gil of course, a rather large young man, and a very salty looking older gentleman, probably in his sixties. Good! No black faces meant no native Bahamians.

Now all there was to do was wait. At around 4PM, we arrived at the hotel parking lot. Our rental van had dark tinting on all windows. We were still worried about Gil spotting us. If he had, he would know immediately what was happening. Just before 5PM a stretch limo that Greg had arranged for, pulled up to the front entrance of the hotel. Five minutes went by and no sign of the crew. Ten more minutes and still nothing.

Then it occurred to us that the limo was parked in front of the hotel entrance, and the marina entrance was somewhat removed from there. So Greg went out in search of a pay phone, and called the limo company. After a few minutes, we observed the limo driver, who had been standing near the car's open trunk, close the trunk and back the car to the head of the marina's main dock. Sure enough, Gil and crew, all neatly dressed, appeared carrying overnight bags, and got aboard the limo.

Off they went, and when they passed our van we all ducked down out of sight.

Now we all hurried down to the boat, carrying all of our gear, provisions and spare diesel. We sounded the tanks and found that Gil had topped off the diesel earlier that day. Then a quick look around found some interesting things. We found personal effects of the crew. The older gentleman's name was Jack Levine according to a passport in that name, along with a GPS receiver that seemed to belong to him. The other young man's name was George, found on some clothing of his.

Greg now called the hotel in Boca and asked to speak with the Johnson party. Well, while room reservations had been made in Gil's name, he had been instructed by the limo driver to wait in the hotel's bar for the film crew to arrive from a shoot in Orlando. Greg told the desk clerk that the Johnson party could be found in the cocktail lounge.

"I'm sorry," the desk clerk replied "The cocktail lounge has been closed for renovations, so the Johnson party has checked into their respective rooms." Well, we had not intended for that to happen. We had planned to tell them of the repossession before they checked in. The room rates were over $400 a night each!

Greg then asked to be connected to Gil's room and somehow ended up talking to Jack Levine instead. "Jack," Greg said "My name is Greg Brazier and I am the rightful owner of the Schooner PHOENIX. I have just legally repossessed the vessel and will be returning her to New York. I see that you have some personal items on board, They will all be returned to you from New York in due time."

After a long pause, Levine said "Does this mean that there will not be an MTV video?"

"I don't know anything about a video," Greg said, "all I know is that I have seized the boat and will have her sailed to New York. I have alerted the Coast Guard of these proceedings, and any attempt to retake the vessel will be met with armed force."

"Oh…" was all that he could say.

By this time, the crew and I had the boat ready to go back to sea, had paid the slip fee, said goodbye to Greg, and headed out of Port Everglades. The plan was to stay outside of the ICW for a while. We did not want Gil to spot us traveling past their hotel.

Upon a closer inspection of Gil's papers, I found a copy of an executed contract leasing PHOENIX to the water sports concession, where she had been working, for the period of one year. That raised a little concern for me. Here we were off shore, and not far from the Bahamas. I envisioned a sport fisherman loaded with machete carrying Bahamians appearing over the horizon ready to take possession of what they felt was legally theirs!

Time to head back to the ICW for safety, after all we were well past Boca by now, so we headed for the inlet at Fort Pierce. Once inside, we confronted yet another dilemma. How tall was our rig? Gil and I had rigged the main topmast last season, and now we had no idea what our air-draft was! All the fixed bridges on the Atlantic ICW, save one, have a minimum vertical clearance of 65 feet, but how high was the top of the main topmast?

Rodney volunteered to climb to the main cross trees for a closer look at the topmast. With much trepidation, we crept up to the first fixed bridge which was just north of Fort Pierce. As bad luck would have it, there was a following tide with a rather strong current pushing us toward the bridge. When we were at the "no turning back point", Rodney yelled down that we would just make it, probably just by inches! Thereafter, we would have no worries about fixed bridges, and had an uneventful trip as far as St. Augustine where we anchored out for the night.

The next morning we opted to go back out to sea since the Georgia ICW is very winding and tricky in spots. Note: PHOENIX was not fitted with a depth sounder, so negotiating uncertain waters was a bit of a stretch.

At sea we picked up a passenger! A lost city pigeon had wandered too far off shore, and was delighted to find a place to rest and to hook a ride. He was quite tame but when we offered him some bread, he declined. So we offered him a drink of fresh water. He could not see the clear water in a clear bowl, so he again declined. After we splashed the water around so that he could see it, he drank and drank for five minutes and then ate all the bread we had set out! Then Pidge decided to explore his new, albeit temporary, home. He flew to the top of the pilot house and stood facing the wind for a long time. Then he flew down into the open focsil and sat on one of the bunks for a while. He stayed with us until we put in to Charleston. When we passed the Battery in the inner harbor, he spotted a flock of his own kind, bade us goodbye and flew off.

We spent a couple of days in Charleston, and had to say goodbye to Art who needed to fly back to Connecticut for business.

When leaving Charleston harbor, we re-entered the ditch and were confronted with the Ben Sawyer Swing bridge which was closed due to a traffic accident on the bridge. We were informed, via VHF radio, that the bridge would be closed to river traffic indefinitely. We were able to find a small marina nearby, and spent the night there.

The next morning saw us headed north once more. It was very uneventful until we got to North Carolina, and the Great Bridge Lock. We had no VHF radio to call the lock tender (we had accidentally left our only radio on the shore side charging unit in Coinjock the previous night) but we made it into the lock by following other traffic.

Once in the lock, we were literally locked into place until we were to be released at the up-river side. As we sat there unable to move, who showed up but Big George, Gil's large crew member. He came up to the boat looking very angry indeed.

"You people have a lot of stuff that belongs to me," he shouted.

It should be said here that during our trip, we had carefully inventoried all of the former crew's belongings and stored them in a number of black garbage bags in the ship's hold.

"Please come aboard and claim anything that belongs to you or Jack. You can have it all except for what belongs to Gil. All you need to do is sign a receipt for what you take"

Somewhat mollified, he went on to say. "I don't know what your beef with Johnson is, whatever it is I had no part in it."

"I know that," I replied, "and I'm sorry that you got caught in the repossession. By the way, how did you pay your way out of the hotel?"

"Of course Johnson had no money, and Jack had only a few bucks, so I had to put over $1200 on my credit card!"

"Good luck getting anything back from Gil," I said, "I'm afraid you're stuck."

George, by now, was no longer angry with us and said to me "Bob, I can see why you did what you had to in order to get PHOENIX back, and I must admit you pulled off a very clever scam to accomplish that. I just wish I had been on the other end!"

With the meeting with Big George, it became obvious that Gil had been following our progress from the land, and George confirmed that.

After leaving Great Bridge we proceeded to Tidewater Marine in Portsmouth, Virginia and took a slip. At this time, Rodney needed to return to Connecticut, and I arranged for a replacement for him, one Escott Smith, a good friend and sailer. The plan was for my wife Sue to drive Escott to Portsmouth and then to give Rodney a ride home. So we had a couple of days wait for her to arrive.

At one point, while I was ashore in the marina's showers, I happened to glance out a shore side window and who should I see wandering about outside, but Gil! I ran down the dock to PHOENIX and warned Rodney that Gil was around, and that we could not leave the boat unattended for even a moment. I was shaken by this development, but when I thought more about it I realized that, of course Gil would never have

PHOENIX heading home

the guts to confront us, let alone try to seize the boat. He was just keeping tabs on our progress.

Later that day Sue arrived with Escott and we all had dinner at the marina's restaurant, then Sue and I spent the night in the adjoining hotel. The next day Sue and Rodney left by car, and Escott and I sailed north.

With one notable exception, the rest of the trip north was uneventful. When we arrived at Schaefer's Canal House in Chesapeake city on the C&D canal, we saw a large sailing vessel belonging to a youth sailing program tied up there. The tide was strong on our stern, so we would have to turn 180 degrees in order to dock up stream. I opted to make the turn opposite the moored vessel. There was a light breeze on our starboard side when we turned. After half way into the turn, the breeze freshened and was now on our port side and began to push us onto the other boat. We almost made it clear, but not quite! Our starboard upper shroud clipped the end of their bowsprit. Unfortunately at that moment, a crew member of Vista was out on the bowsprit! She was not hurt, but was badly frightened. Damage to the bowsprit was one small padeye sheared off. Damage to PHOENIX was a broken spreader on the starboard side. It came crashing down to the deck. The shroud was still intact, but slack without the spreader. Later we took up the slack and all was OK. In the meantime, as soon as we were secured to the dock I went over to the other boat and apologized, asking what the damage was. The captain was very understanding, and said the only damage was the missing padeye, and we need not worry about it. I was, however very shaken up thinking of what might have happened to the girl on the bowsprit had we hit her! How many times have I relived that scene in my head!

Later that evening, Escott and I went ashore to the Canal House Restaurant for dinner. I decided to call home to update Sue on our progress. The restaurant had a tiny room fitted with two pay phones side by side for the public. While I was on one phone, a woman who appeared to be the mate of the boat that we hit came in and made a call on the other one. We were standing side by side at the phones. The mate had not seen me before so didn't know who I was. She called her home base and proceeded to tell whoever that some jerk had hit their boat earlier. I was mortified, quickly finished my call and left the restaurant!

From Chesapeake City to Glen Cove was uneventful and we were glad to see the end of this journey. I met with Greg Brazier and turned the PHOENIX over to him, as per our earlier agreement. He offered me a job as captain to run the PHOENIX out of Glen Cove, but I declined, not wanting to commute from Connecticut.

A week or so later, I ran into Gil at the Black Seal in Essex. He held out his hand saying, "Bob, I just want to say I have no hard feelings toward you for the PHOENIX affair."

I declined to shake hands and said "YOU have no hard feeling? YOU who stole more than $30,000 from me? You're something Johnson, a liar, and a thief!"

That was that for the time being, but a week or so later he showed up at the Black Seal and said he had something to show me. It was a copy of a letter addressed to Greg and copied to me, prepared by a law firm for whom Gil's sister was an attorney, The gist of the letter was that Gil was suing Greg and me for the illegal seizure of the vessel PHOENIX, pursuant with Florida Law. The suit named a sum of $250,000 in damages from both Greg and myself. Knowing what a con artist and liar Gil was, I had no doubt that the letter was total hogwash, I told him as much and ignored the threat. Needless to say, nothing ever came of it.

Thus ends the saga except to say that when the story became widely known around Essex, Gil was largely disgraced, as evidenced by the fact that he was asked to never return to the Black Seal, the favorite watering hole for Essex sailors.

A CRUISING LOG OF EIDOLON

October 2002 through May 2003

MY WIFE SUZANNE AND I had been sailing in EIDOLON, a Henry Scheel designed 37 foot Stonington motorsailer for several years in and around New England's waters. I had made several trips up and down the East Coast, mostly via the Atlantic Intracoastal Waterway in other people's boats and harbored a long time dream of taking our own boat, and my wife for a similar trip.

At this time Sue was winding down the responsibilities of her job as a Vice President in the consumer research department at Saatchi And Saatchi Advertising in New York and I was free from any job ties, so we spent some time planning a six month, give or take, trip to Florida and back.

EIDOLON is a well found motor sailor with a spacious main saloon and galley, and a forward head. The galley is equipped with a two burner propane stovetop, a microwave oven, and a dormitory style refrigerator which runs on 110 volt power supplied by six golf cart batteries and a 1500 watt inverter. A roomy enclosed cockpit served well in bad weather, and was ideal for dining out. Aft finds a very comfortable sleeping cabin with two over sized berths, large hanging locker, and a bank of wonderful built in bureau drawers. Also a full head with shower, (which I had installed).

EIDOLON and DEVNET at Offshore East Marina

EIDOLON'S power is an eighty horse four cylinder Ford engine marinized by BARR. I have rebuilt the lower end of the engine on two different occasions. (I won't go into the reasons for the rebuilds at this time.) Also in the engine room is a fresh water heater, fresh water pressure system, water and fuel tankage.

The Trip

LATE IN OCTOBER OF 2002, the trip began. Sue was called to the west coast for business so I would start without her. Peter Farlekas and Tim Phillips would serve as crew until she could join me. The three of us left on a very blustery morning from Island Cove Marina in Old Saybrook, CT.

The following log entries describe our first few days out:

10/26/02 _____

Destination:	City Island, NY
Port of Departure:	Old Saybrook, CT
Port of Arrival:	Westbrook, CT
Guests on Board:	Peter Farlekas, Tim Phillips
Weather Conditions:	Windy, 25 to 35 knots from SW

Got as far as Saybrook Point Light in heavy weather. Were warned by radio not to come out into the sound. Returned to Island Cove. Will try again later in the day.

Tried again in the afternoon, winds down somewhat but still blowing hard. Decided to put into Westbrook Ct. at about 1600 hours. Roxanne, Peter's wife, picked us up to spend the night at home.

10/27/02 _____

Destination:	City Island NY
Port of Departure:	Westbrook, CT
Port of Arrival:	City Island, NY
Guests on Board:	Ditto
Weather Conditions:	Clear

Weather opposite of yesterday, very nice day, clear, calm.

City Island is a hoot. We had dinner in a restaurant that was featured in a Ben Stiller/Robert De Niro movie. There are apparently no fuel services on City Island, so we had to go over to Manhasset for diesel.

10/28/02

Destination:	Manasquan Inlet, (Brielle, NJ)
Port of Departure:	City Island, NY
Guests on Board:	Ditto
Weather Conditions:	Clear, high overcast, wind NW 10-12 kts.

Brielle is a cute little town. Railroad drawbridge close at hand, very noisy at 4:00 A.M.

Took on 15 gallons diesel, all other fluids O.K. Had a nice dinner at the SANDBAR.

Time to say goodbye to Peter. Wife Roxanne drove to Brielle to bring Pete home. She also brought our bikes. Thank God for the bikes, they were invaluable for the whole cruise.

Going slowly up the river

10/29/02 _____

Destination:	Atlantic City, NJ
Port of Departure:	Manasquan Inlet (Brielle, NJ)
Port of Arrival:	Atlantic City, NJ
Guests on Board:	Tim Phillips
Weather Conditions:	Wind 25–30 kts NE

We were taking a beating outside so decided to try the New Jersey ICW for a while. Put in to Barnegat inlet at 1000 hrs. The inside route in Jersey is not particularly nice, but at least it was calm. We arrived at Trump's place (marina) at 1600 hours, in time to go ashore for dinner at Hooters in the casino. Slippage here is steep, $4.50/foot!

In a previous trip down the New Jersey ICW, I had encountered a temporary glitch in the route. It seemed that a section of the ditch had shoaled to the point of being impassable, so a detour was charted. The detour involved a fixed bridge with vertical clearance of 25 feet! On this trip I was in a 36 foot power boat, rather than sail, so the bridge was not a problem.

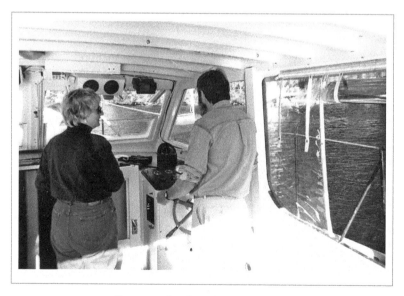

Skipper and wife in the ample cockpit

Now EIDOLON has an airdraft of around 49 feet, so we could be facing a problem if we continued down the ICW, as we would have liked, since conditions outside were fierce. Solution: I called Coast Guard Station Absecon and asked if the detour was still in effect. I was told, no, the channel had been cleared, and the low bridge was no longer a problem. We were clear to go. I thanked the Coasties, and we set out in the AM bound for Cape May.

10/30/02 _____

Destination:	Cape May, NJ
Port of Departure:	Atlantic City, NJ
Port of Arrival:	Cape May, NJ
Guests on Board:	Ditto
Weather Conditions:	Wild outside, overcast and raining inside.

After proceeding for about 10 miles, we encountered a drawbridge. There are millions of them on the New Jersey ICW. When I called the bridge for an opening, a boater downstream, hearing my call, called and asked if we were going all the way to Cape May. I replied that we were.

Skipper and wife on the aft deck

He then came back with the news that another bridge further down was closed for repairs and would not be operating for at least another week! So much for Coast Guard information.

So we headed back to Atlantic City and punched out into some very heavy seas. Arrived Cape May late afternoon and put into Utch's Marine for the night.

10/31/02

Destination:	Chesapeake City, MD
Port of Departure:	Cape May, NJ
Port of Arrival:	Chesapeake City, MD
Guests on Board:	Ditto
Weather Conditions:	Choppy in Delaware Bay, winds 15 kts NW

Got thru the Cape May Canal early on and then into Delaware Bay. Pounding into the chop in the Bay, making 6-7 knots with ebbing tide. Arrived Schaefer's Canal House at 1700 hours. Had dinner ashore, put on 13 gallons diesel, one quart lube oil. Engine hours 942.

Schaefer's Canal House seems to be in a state of decline since the last time I was there. Portions of the dock are closed and look to be falling apart!

11/01/02

Destination:	Baltimore, MD
Port of Departure:	Chesapeake City, MD
Port of Arrival:	Baltimore, MD, Harbor View Marina
Guests on Board:	Ditto
Weather Conditions:	Sunny, breezy, choppy, wind 15-20 NW.

Starboard side windshield wiper stopped working in heavy spray situation. Alternator o/p to tach came adrift. Broken wire. Took on 15 gallons diesel.

We had to replace the helm side (starboard) with the port side windshield wiper so that the helmsman could see where he was going. We repaired the alternator o/p to the tach but still seemed to have a problem. Possibly a slipping belt? We will check further at a later date.

A problem was developing with the pressure water system. The tank seemed to be "burping" and the system was not being fully charged. Again, we will check this problem out later.

11/02/02 _____

Destination:	Annapolis, MD
Port of Departure:	Baltimore, MD
Port of Arrival:	Annapolis, MD
Guests on Board:	Ditto
Weather Conditions:	Clear, winds W 10-12

I planned to stay here for the better part of a week. Tim had to leave so we rented a car for him to drive home. Sue was finishing up her assignment in California, and the plan called for her to drive Tim's rental car back to Annapolis when she got home, in a week.

I spent part of the time there checking out the alternator problem. It turned out that the pivot bolt on the alternator mount had sheared off, leaving the alternator more or less hanging. Replacing the bolt was an easy repair. On checking the pressure water system, I discovered an engine control cable was interfering with the pressure switch on the water pump. Again, a very easy fix.

After cleaning up minor problems, I had the better part of a week to explore Annapolis, mostly by bike. It's a great town and I had a ball. Visited the U.S. Naval Academy where I had a guided tour, very interesting. Went to the local Marriott Hotel where there is the 12 foot model of the African Queen on display in the lobby. The model had been used for filming the white water scenes in the movie. I met the innkeeper who owns the model, and told him of my experiences with the real Queen, he was very interested in hearing about Jim Hendrix and his antics on the Connecticut River!

At the end of the week, Sue arrived in the rental car. She called me and asked for directions to the marina where I was staying. She was shaken up because just before she called, a rather large limb fell out of a tree she was driving under! She was concerned that when we returned the car, they would notice that the rental agreement did not include her as one of the drivers, and that along with the tree limb damage, could be expensive. Not to worry, there really was no noticeable damage, and no one noticed that she was not Tim Phillips the driver.

From this point in the narrative, I will dispense with listing the formal log entries, but will be guided by them in the writing.

NOW THAT SUE WAS BACK, I felt as if our cruise was finally starting. We spent one more day in Annapolis so Sue could see some of the city, then it was time to move on.

11/08/02

We had a very nice day down the Bay to Solomons Island, MD. Winds were SW at 10-12 knots. We took a slip at Calvert Marine. We had been there previously and liked the place. Borrowed a loaner car, an ancient Mercedes, and did some grocery shopping in town.

11/09/02

We left Solomons early and headed out for Deltaville, VA. The Bay was decidedly lumpy with a SW breeze of 15 knots. Later in the day, the wind subsided, but the seas were still lumpy and we both got tired of being banged about.

At Deltaville we put into Fishing Bay Harbour and took a slip. This is a very nice marina with very good facilities. Next to the marina is Deagles Boat Yard which was in the process of re-planking a large portion of the Trumpy PRINCIPIA of Philadelphia. I was surprised to see that happening, since she had undergone a large overhaul less than 10 years earlier at Billings Diesel in Maine.

We had planned to spend just one night in Fishing Bay, but the morning of 11/10/02 brought dense fog so we opted for a layday.

At about this time, the pressure water system, which had always been flaky, decided that it wanted to be replaced. Luckily there is a West Marine store within biking distance of the marina, so I bought a new water pump and accumulator tank. This new arrangement was far superior to the old system, and served us well up to the time when we sold EIDOLON.

The following day NOAA was calling for waterspouts in the Bay, so we decided for yet another layday. It was proving fun not having to adhere to a schedule, but to just roll with the flow. Bob got a flat tire on his bike coming back from West Marine, had to push the bike back in the pouring rain.

11/13/02 _____

When leaving Fishing Bay Harbour it's a long way out to the Bay. Just look at the chart!

Once outside, we hit the first of a series of rollers for which we were not prepared. I had forgotten to dog the refer door, and soon the entire contents of same were scattered around the galley sole. Big mess!

Made it to Tidewater Marine in Portsmouth by 1700 hours, in the rain. We had an awful time trying to see out the windshield in the rain. Bought some RAINX in the ship's store and will apply in the morning. Had dinner at the marina's restaurant, it was very nice.

11/14/02 _____

We got a late start leaving Tidewater Marine, knowing we were only going as far as Coinjock, NC this day. Also, one of the Elizabeth River lift bridges does not operate until 0800 hrs. (We found that out on a previous trip when arrived at the bridge at 0600 hours and had to hold position for 2 hours!)

Going down the Elizabeth River we saw EMMA B at Atlantic Yachts. She looked great!

Coinjock is a delightful stop on the Virginia Cut, just south of Great Bridge Lock. The first time I saw Coinjock was in '89, just a sleepy little backwater. Now she looks quite different, with several new marinas, but still nice.

We had a nice dinner on board and went for a quiet walk afterwards.

11/15/02 _____

Set off early bound for the Alligator River. Day starts with dense fog, but it lifted by the time we got to Albemarle Sound. We had a nice sail, first in a long time, across the Sound. Wind 20 knots from the nw. Should have tied in a reef but didn't.

Found a nice anchorage up the river from the swing bridge before the Pungo Canal. Very quiet, with two other boats there. I fixed my bike's flat tire here, very easy as it was the front tire. Had a peaceful night, still fairly warm.

11/16/02 _____

Hauled anchor at 0800 hours and headed down the Pungo Canal, bound for Belhaven, NC. The canal is straight as a die, and was perfect for final tuning of the radar. In heads up mode, we just shot straight down the canal.

Made River Forest Marina in early afternoon amid heavy rain and severe overcast. We were sorry to hear that Enoch had retired as dock master, but a nice young gal had taken his place, and was very intrigued with EIDOLON. Always nice to be appreciated. Enoch called the marina when we were there, happy in retirement, baking apple pies!

Decided on a layday, borrowed a golf cart and went to the local hardware store in the rain, fun. Met a nice couple on FREAY'S POND, a 46 foot steel ketch. She a Canadian and he a retired British nuclear sub engineer. They are on their way to Cuba to attend her daughter's wedding.

Buffet dinner in the antebellum mansion was disappointing. It has gone down hill from the old days that I remembered. Apparently the former owner had died and left his widow and two sons to run the place. One, or both, of the sons was/were more interested in partying than running a marina. Same sort of fate as Schaefer's Canal House suffered. What a shame!

10/18/02 _____

We set sail for Oriental, NC early in the AM. Nice breezy day, winds 10-12 from the NW. Pamlico sound calm, flat. Arrived Oriental early in the afternoon.

Oriental, the self proclaimed sailing capital of North Carolina, is a wonderful place. Very friendly people. We biked all over the place. Met Pastor Jim Ransom who is a fan of Stonnington Motor Sailers. We took yet another lay day, and when returning to the dock after sightseeing, we were surprised to see that EMMA B had arrived. We had a nice get together and dined ashore with John and Emma Angier.

11/20/02 _____

The next morning EMMA B left early. We stayed until lunchtime, then left for Minnesott Beach where we planned to leave EIDOLON and go home for the holidays.

The marina at Minnesott Beach is buried in the woods! You couldn't ask for a better hurricane hole. People there were very friendly. We found ourselves in a pot luck supper with tons of food, none of which came from us, as we had emptied our refer for the month.

Met up with Jim Ransom and his wife. They took us out for ice cream and coffee. Very friendly people. We have fond memories of Minnesott Beach.

11/22/02

Changed the oil with a new drain oil pump that worked very well. Will haul out tomorrow with instructions to the yard to scrape and paint the bottom and replace zincs, then took a cab to New Bern to rent a car for the trip home.

11/23/02 - 12/28/02

Home for the Holidays.

12/29/02

Spent Sunday night at the Best Western in Norfolk, and arrived at Minnesott Beach at 2:00 PM. to find EIDOLON back in the water. All appeared to be OK, but the marina was now deserted. Below deck there was a huge amount of condensation! Cushions were soaked, books were damp.

While Sue was cleaning up below, a hose clamp let go on the pressure water system, and the pressure pump emptied the water tanks. Unfortunately the water had been turned off at the dock so filling the empty tanks was a chore. We formed a bucket brigade from the one working spigot at the far side of the marina. It took a while!

Settled up for the bottom painting and zincs - $349.

12/31/02

Calm, warm, partly overcast for the trip to Beaufort, NC. Beaufort is a very pretty little town, with several marinas right on Front Street. We took a slip at Beaufort Docks Marina ($1.25/foot) and borrowed a wreck of a loaner to go grocery shopping at a PAK-N-SAK. Cute store.

We had a nice New Year's Eve dinner ashore, then back to the boat to watch Jay Leno on TV. Spent New Year's Day right there, resting.

1/02/03 _____

Left Beaufort in rain, light fog bound for New River, NC. Condensation on the windshield a problem. Ran for a while at 2200 RPM to make the draw bridge at Onslow Beach. Engine temperature was up to 180 degrees. Normally runs at 150-155 degrees.

New River is not really a marina, just a fuel dock with cheapest fuel on the ICW according to Skipper Bob - $1.00/gallon. We stayed at the fuel dock for the night for $.50/foot. No electric or water. We noticed here that the VCR does not work well on batteries, and the microwave took 4-5 minutes to heat a mug of coffee. Something is wrong here. It will take a long time to figure out that one!

1/03/03 _____

Left New River in clear, breezy weather bound for Wrightsville Beach.

Missed Surf City swing bridge, ½ hour wait.

Missed Figure Eight Island swing bridge, ½ hour wait.

Missed Wrightsville bascule bridge, 1 hour wait.

If we could cruise at 8-9 knots we would not have so many bridge delays, but at 6-7 knots, we get caught. Wrightsville Beach is nice. Stayed at the Bridge Tender Marina, just south of the bridge. Biked into town and tried out our new saddle bags which were very helpful. Had nice dinner ashore.

1/04/03 _____

Morning brings a clear sunny day for the trip to Southport, NC. Made 12 knots down the Cape Fear River with the tide!

Southport would become one of our favorite spots on the ICW. We took our bikes to a hardware store and bought a stepstool for ease in boarding the boat. The bikes are turning out to be a real Godsend for shoreside transportation.

Sue finally got online with the marina's WI-FI !

We put in two loads of laundry, only to find that the driers were not working. Had to take all that wet wash back onboard for the next stop. We spent one more layday here.

1/05/03 _____

We left Southport for Cricket Cove Marina in Little River, SC. Lovely day, warm 55 degrees.

We arrived at Cricket Cove at low tide. Very nice new docks, but NO WATER. We had to plow into our slip at full throttle! Other than that, a nice place to stay the night. Sue was able to get online again in the boaters lounge. Took our bikes to the local CVS for supplies. This is not a good place to bike. The only way to CVS was Rt. 17, with lots of traffic and no shoulder for bikes. Harrowing!

Lost ship's 110 power. Turned out that all the golf cart batteries were low on water. Topped them off and will check again tomorrow after a full charge.

1/06/03 _____

Left Cricket Cove at 8:30 AM bound for Waca Wachee Marina on the Wacamaw River. Nice day, warm, 61 degrees. Passed by Bucksport, SC where Sue took many pictures. Bucksport, formerly Bucksville, was founded by an ancestor of mine, one Capt. Henry Buck, son of Col. Jonathan Buck of Bucksport Maine, my great great great great great grandfather. Bucksport, SC seems much busier than when I was last there, fourteen years earlier.

Waca Wachee Marina is very nice. We borrowed the courtesy car and went shopping. Mikey, the marina's yellow lab was very friendly, buck teeth and all.

While we watched, a large, 50+ foot motor yacht put in for the night. The crew seemed somewhat overwhelmed with the boat, but managed to eventually get landed.

1/07/03 _____

Left for Georgetown, SC on a clear breezy cool morning. The trip down the Wacamaw through the cypress swamp was breathtakingly beautiful.

Arrived in Georgetown in time for lunch at The Rice Paddy. Very good! Visited Augustus and Caroline Antiques and took in the Kaminsky House. Strolled the boardwalk, and took in lots of shops. After we were secured to the dock, the large motor yacht that we had seen at Waca Wachee arrived and attempted to dock just ahead of us. Our previous feeling that the crew was green was made apparent with this docking procedure. With much gunning of engines, some shouting and an eventual crunching involving our bow pulpit, they got her tied up. Damage to us was minor, but the embarrassment factor for them was huge.

Had dinner aboard. Very cold and windy. We decided to leave in the AM as a wind shift had made the presence of the local paper mill all too obvious. In spite of all that, we sort of fell in love with Georgetown, and would eventually return on more than one occasion.

1/08/03 _____

A cool and breezy day to Isle of Palms marina, just north of Charleston. Had to push hard to arrive by 1700 hours.

Very nice marina with lots of friendly rednecks around the docks. Sue was able to get on-line in the dockmaster's office. She got caught up with a lot of banking, etc. Dinner on board.

1/09/03 _____

Left Isle of Palms bound for Bohicket Marine. Breezy but warm day. Went past Charleston, very pretty from the water, lots of church spires.

When we got to marker #110, we realized that Bohicket Marine was considerably out of the way of our route, and since it was already 1600 hours, we decided to anchor in Steamboat Creek for the night. What a lovely anchorage! We had it to ourselves and enjoyed watching several boats going by. As they passed #110, instead of turning right for the ICW, they would continue straight down the North Edisto River. A half an hour later, after they realized their mistake, we would see them chugging back up the river, then re-entering the ICW at #110. Fun!

Spent a very nice evening here, sure to return again sometime.

1/10/03 _____

Left lovely Steamboat Creek at 0900 hours bound for Beaufort, SC.

Lady's Island Bridge was closed in the AM but was repaired in time for our 1400 opening.

Beaufort is a very pretty antebellum town. I was here years before and fell in love with it then. We had dinner at Plums, nice but very (too) noisy.

Made some repairs in the galley, new sink faucet, etc. Laid over for another day. Borrowed loaner car and did some sight seeing, even went over to Lady's island, against the rules for the loaner car. It seems that some time ago, boaters had taken the car to Lady's Island. Then the bridge got stuck in the open position for two days before the loaner could make it back!

1/12/03 _____

Left Beaufort on a partly cloudy, breezy and cool day, headed for Hilton Head. Port Royal Sound was very lumpy, but the rest of the day was fine.

My sister in-law Sandra met us at the dock in Harbour Town. Very nice facility. Spent a layday with Sandra. Bought and installed all new golf cart batteries! (Someday I will find out what is going on with our battery situation!).

Had dinner the first night at brother Dick's and Sandra's, the second night at Truffles with Sandra. Dick was not feeling well. I'm afraid Dick is not doing very well, he has slowed down a lot, and has to stop to catch his breath too often.

I have had to add ATF fluid now on an almost daily basis.

1/14/03 _____

Said goodbye to Dick and Sandra and left for Thunderbolt, GA. NIce warm day, no wind. Took a slip at Palmer Johnson. No fuel here due to dock repairs. Also no cable TV and lousy hot water in the showers. They turned off electricity at our dock before we left. But, true to tradition, we had the newspaper and Crispy Creme delivered in the morning.

Will spend a layday here. Rented an Enterprise car and went sight seeing. Downtown Savannah, Skidaway Island, Isle of Hope, Tybee Island and Fort Pulaski.

1/16/03 _____

Left Thunderbolt for Hampton River Marina. Clear, cool, breezy day.

Discovered an error in the Waterway Guide. The guide reported Hampton River Marina at MM 635. It is actually at MM 665. No way to make that before dark, so we anchored in Tea Kettle Creek. Excellent anchorage, we had it to ourselves. Very starry night with no land lights to interfere.

1/17/03 _____

Left early for Fernandina Beach Harbor Marina. Cool, breezy, overcast in the AM, cleared in the afternoon.

Saw seven or eight wild horses on Cumberland Island, beautiful! Met Harry and Ellen Moles on TUFFY II, very nice people, had them over for wine and cheese.

Fernandina is a beautiful town, lots to do and see. Rode our bikes out to Fort Clinch. Very interesting, will visit it again in the spring.

On Friday we got word that the Sister Creek Bridge, just before the St. John's River was down for maintenance over the weekend, and would not be operational before Monday. That was fine with us, a few more days in Fernandina were welcomed.

Come Sunday morning the wind was up, 25-30 from the west. We were on the face dock, and the westerly wind had us plastered to the dock and chafing badly. Our fenders were not up to the task.

I found a truck tire hanging off the dock some distance away, and hauled it to the boat. In order to get the tire between the dock and the boat, I had to pry the boat off using a ten foot length of 2x6 lumber! It was a trial, but I finally made it and slid the barnacle encrusted tire between the boat and the dock. There was a lot of superficial damage to the port side to be fixed later.

1/20/03 _____

Left Fernandina Tuesday AM. (The Sister Creek bridge was still down Monday AM). When we finally got to the bridge, it was closed to river traffic because some drunk had driven thru one of the roadside barriers, at 0930 hours!, so the bridge could not stop highway traffic to open for us. Four hours later we finally got through. Bound for Whitney's Marina (Up the St. Johns River).

Met up with Trudy and John Lichacz, Ernie and Gene Lopresti. Stayed at Ernie and Gene's on Black Creek. Had a fun time there. Gene and I played with our potato guns, without much success. Mine wouldn't work, and Gene lost some eyebrows to his.

Heard a gruesome story of a young lad who went for a swim in Black Creek not too long ago. Seems he dove into a nest of cottonmouths. He didn't make it!

Met "Fred" and his wonderful, mostly homemade, steel trawler. Fifty feet plus, he's doing a great job on her.

1/22/03 _____

Left Whitney's for St. Augustine on a cool overcast day. The trip down/up? The St. Johns River was very interesting. Lots of bridges and commercial shipping in and around Jacksonville.

Fetched up at the Municipal Marina, right at the foot of King Street. Very nice marina. We stayed here for three nights.

Loved St. Augustine! Biked all over, got a guided tour of Flagler College, did the winery, the Wax Museum, Ripley's Believe it Or Not, Flagler's church, etc., etc. Saw the oldest oak tree, "The Senator" 600 plus years old.

It was cold for our stay here. So cold that all the live-aboards on moorings came into the marina and sacked out in the lounge and laundry room.

1/24/03 _____

Left St. Augustine for Daytona. Short day.

Stayed at the City Marina. I've been there many times before. Very convenient to town. Had KFC takeout for dinner, watched the Super Bowl.

1/25/03 _____

Left Daytona for Titusville. Weather is finally warming up. Winds SW 10-12, clear day.

Wind increased just in time to dock in a *very* tight spot. Got blown all over the place trying to get into a slip. Finally decided to tie up to the face dock. Wise decision!

Met Trudy and John and spent two days ashore with them. Visited the Space Center, very interesting. Trudy thought I was too quiet but in fact I was having a great time. Lots of manatees at the marina. Went shopping at a really bad SAVE-A-LOT. Not impressed with Titusville.

1/30/03 _____

Left Titusville at 0900 hours. Nice day, very calm, sunny and warm. Finally starting to feel like Florida. Headed for Melbourne, biked ashore and I got another flat, front wheel.

1/31/03 _____

Met by Faith and Don Oakes. Don came with me for the trip to Fort Pierce, Sue and Faith drove. Don had a bad cold, but seemed to enjoy the uneventful trip. We spent 3 nights with Don and Faith at their house in Spanish Wells. Left EIDOLON at Harbortown Marina in Fort Pierce. Nice facility. Put in a new holding tank at this time.

2/03/03 _____

Warm day, left for Northside Marina in Port St. Lucie. Shortly after leaving our slip, we smelled strong diesel fumes. A quick look in the engine room revealed diesel spraying all over from a failed petcock on the engine fuel filter. Thank God it wasn't gasoline!

Returned to Harbortown and made emergency repairs. Went to West Marine for parts and could not find a good replacement part, so had to jury rig. We will have to find a better solution later.

Nice warm day for the trip to Port St. Lucie. Entrance to the St. Lucie River is quite confusing, but we made it without incident and took a slip at Northside Marina.

2/04/03 _____

Left Northside early. Beautiful morning, temp close to 80 degrees. Okeechobee waterway is pretty. Had a long wait at the St. Lucie Lock (Up 15 feet). We saw a large alligator while we waited.

Made it to Port Mayaca by early afternoon. Tied off to two dolphins for the night. Met Chris and Dave Scott on board POYANNA, a North-bay 36. Nice boat, nice people. Had wine and cheese on their boat.

2/05/03 _____

Locked up to lake level, about 15 feet, in the AM. Overcast, breezy day. Very lumpy on the lake at first. We had decided to take the rim route rather than the cross lake route. When we got as far as Pahokee, we were protected by spoils islands so the trip was much smoother.

Locked down to Clewiston to spend the night at Roland's Fish Camp. Nice place. Borrowed the marina's van and went with Chris and Dave to have dinner at the Clewiston Inn.

2/06/03 _____

When we left Clewiston, we did not need to lock up. The Clewiston Lock depends on the wind condition on the lake. If the wind is out of the south, the lake is drawn down to the Clewiston level, and the lock is left open, until the wind shifts to the north when the lake level becomes higher than Clewiston. Interesting!

A sunny, warm, actually hot day took us to sleepy little LaBelle, after locking thru Moore Haven and one smaller lock. Had to wait at the Moore Haven Lock while a 200 plus foot American Cruise Line ship went thru. Just enough space in the lock for the one ship.

LaBelle is cute, but decidedly seedy. Took a free slip for the night and biked to town. VERY Mexican!

Called daughter Katie and found she was in bad pain with heartburn. She had to take an ambulance to the hospital! She called back later that evening feeling better. Hope they can get to the bottom of her trouble.

2/07/03 _____

Left LaBelle on a warm and sunny day. Caloosahatchee canal and river are very beautiful. Saw lots of gators on the river bank.

Got to Fort Myers in the early afternoon. Took a mooring at Fort Myers Yacht Basin. $6.00 per night for six nights.

Had a wonderful stay with Sam and Gretch Alessi. Had dinner with Laurie and Warren Meyers twice, once at the Veranda, very nice, very pricey.

Went to a huge flea market with Sam. Fun.

2/13/03 _____

Left Fort Myers for Marco, FL on a sunny, warm day, but very lumpy in the Gulf. Lots of pitching! Sanibel Bridge openings are restricted due to slower vehicular traffic. Word is that the bridge is in very bad shape. Speed limit on the bridge is 10 MPH.

Took a slip at Marco River Marina. Expensive! Took bikes ashore for grocery shopping at Publix. Lots of Bentleys, Mercedes, Jags etc. around town.

2/14/03 _____

Left Marco Island for the Little Shark River in the Everglades. Very nice day, warm, sunny, and no chop today. Got a little confused when leaving, markers seem to make no sense, but made it out alright.

Everglades! Spectacular! Beautiful!

Anchored in The Little Shark River, very serene, wonderful sunset, only 3-4 other boats in the anchorage. Evening sounds from the glades were fantastic. Want to come back someday and really explore the Everglades.

2/15/03 _____

Left Little Shark River on a warm, beautiful morning headed for Marathon, FL. The Everglades were on our port beam most of the day. Touched bottom near passage thru Seven Mile Bridge. Put into City Marina in Marathon. Marcia, and Jim Cousins and their friends Ed and Ann came for drinks on board. Then we all went to Ed and Ann's for supper.

When we returned to EIDOLON we found a business card of Charlie Getchel's in the cockpit, with a note expressing an interest in the boat. I called Charlie and left a message to call. When he finally got back to us, he wanted to know who owned EIDOLON. He was shocked to hear that it was us! He had no idea when he left the card. Turns out he was living aboard at the same marina. We got together for a drink on his old Ray Hunt, which was looking a lot better than the last time we saw her.

Spent one layday here, then on to Key West.

2/17/03 _____

Overcast most of the day, but warm. One rain shower in the afternoon. Put in to Key West Bight Marina.

Had Bill and Lee Brakeman and their friends aboard for a visit and we all went to the Turtle Kraal for drinks. Had dinner with Bill and Lee, and breakfast in the morning.

Went shopping by bike, Key West was it's usual crazy self. Went to Fort Zachery Taylor. Interesting.

Key West, as always, is good for a few days, then it's time to go.

Back to Marathon, Boot Key Harbor.

2/19/03 _____

Very nice day, cloudless. Had wind and tide in our face, but made OK time.

Had Charlie over for a chat. Made spaghetti and sausage for dinner. Bob biked out to Pigeon Key on the seven mile bridge.

2/20/03 _____

Left Boot Key for Islamorada. Sunny and warm, seas lumpy. Rock and roll until Channel Five where we went inside to Florida Bay. Seas calm, but very shoal.

Anchored out using 35 lb CQR. Very large anchorage. Saw TUFFY II, Bob dingeyed over to say hello.

Bob dingeyed ashore and walked miles to the nearest grocery store, will bring bikes ashore soon.

We rigged our huge American flag at the masthead. Very impressive, could be seen for miles! Then I went ashore with the bikes, left them locked up to the mangroves, and returned to the boat.

While I was working in the galley, I happened to look out a porthole, and couldn't see the boat that was anchored next to us. Funny, I didn't see them leave.

Once on deck, I couldn't see any of our neighbors! You guessed it, we were dragging in a stiff breeze, headed for the far side of Florida Bay at 2 - 3 knots.

We got the engine started, retrieved the thoroughly fouled anchor and motored back to our original position, dropped the CQR and then ran our yachtsman down the chain rode for extra holding. It seems that the giant flag had wrapped the backstay and was acting as a very powerful sail! When I thought about what would have happened if I had not gotten back aboard when I did, Sue would have found herself in the Everglades. Later that night, it really started to blow. While we were secure, half the anchorage dragged anchors all over the place. We were lucky not to get run over!

Golf cart batteries not charging properly. We need to run engine every four-five hours. I can't understand what is going on. Alternator is putting out proper voltage. Will find out much later that though the voltage was correct from the alternator, amperage was way low! Meantime, we struggle with low batteries.

Stayed here until the 24th.

02/24/03 _____

Hauling in the anchors turned into a real challenge. When I finally got the yachtsman back aboard, the CQR only came part way up using the windless. I struggled and moaned and finally got the CQR to the surface, only to discover it had fouled an old, very old, barnacle encrusted abandoned anchor chain of some size. Working with the boat hook I got the mess untangled after a while, and we were free at last to leave and headed for Gilbert's Resort and Fish Camp in Key Largo.

Gilbert's is very nice. Located near the drawbridge at Jewfish Creek. Very friendly place.

We rented a car from Enterprise and went shopping for new golf cart batteries and installed them.

Received the awful news that our friend Bill Novotny died in St. John USVI. If we had not been on this cruise, we would have been in St. John with Bill and Ayn!

Sue had fun feeding a very tame manatee.

2/27/03 _____

Left Gilbert's at 0900 bound for Tarpon Basin anchorage. Fine day. Anchored near Quay restaurant, dingeyed ashore, walked to Publix. Long walk!

Nice anchorage, set two anchors. Not much water here. Batteries holding out. Quiet evening.

2/28/03 _____

Left Tarpon Basin for Buttonwood Sound.

Nice anchorage near Snooks. Spent three nights here, very nice. Biked all over the place. Had to run engine one hour in five.

3/02/03 _____

Back to Gilbert's for one night. Biked to West Marine for fuses. Left all hatches open. Then guess what? Black clouds overhead and torrential downpour!

When we got back to the boat, all was soaked. Duvets in the aft cabin included. Wet, they weighed about 10 pounds apiece. It took lots of quarters in the laundry room to dry out.

Met up again with Bob and Linda on their G-36 and Barbara and Jack on their Navigator 37. Bob is very funny. Remember about apologizing to the Puerto Ricans?

3/03/03 _____

Left Gibert's for the last time, headed for Dinner Key. Hot and hazy day. Took a slip at the City Marina, next to Jimmy Johnson's THREE RINGS sportfish.

Biked to the "Grove", and had a nice dinner at the Cheesecake Factory. The place is loaded with Cubans!

As nice as the area is, it's also loaded with homeless, who will try anything to get into the marina. You have to watch out and not buy their stories about having lost their key!

3/04/03 _____

Left Miami for Lauderdale. Nice day but very hot and humid.

Took a slip at Bahia Mar. Nice as usual.

Called Paul Mathews and will meet him tomorrow on Singer Island.

Left Bahia Mar bound for an anchorage at Lantana. Hot and humid, 80 degrees.

Went aground just south of Lantana. Chart confusing here. Couldn't motor off so I prepared to kedge us off. I had tied the dink off under the bow and had dropped the CQR into it to set the anchor in deep water within the channel. At about this time, the sheriff appeared in a cigarette and asked if we wanted a pull off. I said sure and handed them a line and he got the job done in a jiff.

Sue was near panic when the sheriff showed up because I had filled her head with stories of major fines for grounding in protected waters in Florida. Fortunately the Lantana area does not contain protected areas.

Went ashore for dinner at The Old Keylime Restaurant, very nice.

3/06/03 _____

Left Lantana for North Palm Beach Marina. Nice marina.

Paul Mathews and wife showed up and took us out for dinner. My birthday dinner, very nice of them.

Biked to Riviera Beach for Sue's medicine. Went past the old trailer park where Shelly, Sue's father, spent the winter. Brought back memories.

Talked to Rodney by phone. He is fine, living on Great Cranberry Island Maine.

3/09/03 _____

Left North Palm Beach for Jensen Beach, Nettles Island.

Nettles Island is a square shaped spoils island, and is packed with vacation cottages. Neat place! Lots of very friendly people, cute store and restaurant with good food. We walked across Hutchinson Island to a really great beach.

3/11/03 _____

Left Nettles Island for Vero Beach.

Boy do we love Vero (Velcro) Beach! City Marina charges $8.50 per night for a mooring.

Met up with Ted and Lori again. Their trip to Cuba was not fun. The harbor where they were to stay for the wedding did not have enough water for their boat, so they had to anchor out in unprotected water. Ted had to stay aboard for three days during a blow. Then officials came aboard and hassled Ted until he had to bribe them!

Vero has a free bus service for all around town, great for shopping.

Had dinner with Ted and Lori. Then with Faith and Don, and then with Pete and Bobbie Ameno.

Battery problems continue, bought an extra for backup.

Hated to leave Vero.

3/16/03 _____

Left Vero for Diamond 99 Marina. (Log does not say where this is?)

Tiny marina with only one transient slip. Not much water either, had to winch ourselves into a slip. Marina has a schipperke mascot.

Met Dave and Betty on their Gulfstar 43. They did a great job on converting it to a trawler, complete with outrigger stabilizers.

Thunderstorm in the afternoon.

3/17/03

Left Diamond 99 for Titusville Municipal Marina.

Saw lots of Manatees at the marina. Biked to town and shopped at that really bad SAV-A-LOT.

Violent thunderstorms in the afternoon/evening.

3/18/03

Left Titusville for Daytona.

Nicest day of the winter, warm and dry with a cooling breeze. Had dinner with Trudy and John.

3/19/03

Left Daytona for St. Augustine. Warm and humid, rained when we got to St. Augustine.

Rained off and on all afternoon, but we had a nice stay. Had lunch at Alcazar Cafe. We love that place!

Visited Flagler's church in time for choir practice. Very impressive.

3/20/03

Left St. Augustine for Fernandina. Severe thunderstorm in the morning. Had to stop till rain passed, couldn't see anything in the downpour.

Got to Fernandina in the late afternoon. Had dinner in the Florida House Inn. Wonderful old world hospitality.

3/21/03

Left Fernandina for Brunswick. Plan to stay at Brunswick Landing Marina for the better part of a month. We love this place and had a wonderful time there. Got a lot done on the boat.

Norm's dink that we had been using bit the dust getting stuck under a floating dock. Tried to repair it with Crazy Glue, but no good.

Harry called to say that Ellen is off the boat and home in Columbia. She had a bad fall on TUFFY II and injured her back. Sad!

4/11/03 _____

Left Brunswick for Kilkenny Creek. First nice day in five. Kilkenny Creek is very country and very buggy. Had dinner on POLLYANA.

4/12/03 _____

Left Kilkenny Creek early, bound for Hilton Head. Very nice day. Arrived at Harbour Town at 1430.

Had dinner and spent the night at Dick and Sandra's.

Dick does not look at all well. COPD is catching up with him I'm afraid!

4/13/03 _____

Left HH on a lovely day for a short trip to Beaufort, SC. We still love this wonderful town.

Had dinner ashore with Chris and Dave.

4/14/03 _____

Another lovely day for the trip to Steamboat Creek. Arrived at 1530. Had dinner aboard.

4/15/03 _____

Steamboat Creek to Charleston. Took a slip at the Maritime Center on the Cooper River. Neat place but you really rock and roll here from commercial boat traffic

The Scotts are also here and we both took laydays.

Great shopping here all within walking distance. Watched a frisbee game in the park. They had the cutest little teacup yorkie!

Went to the nearby IMAX theater for a spectacular film about the Antarctic.

4/17/03 _____

Left Charleston for Georgetown. Very long day. Had the tide against us almost all day. Took a slip at Georgetown Landing Marina. Slippage was $.50/foot more than Skipper Bob reported. Also, Bob said cable was available here. Turned out not for transients, only regular customers.

Gear box appears to be still leaking.

4/18/03 _____

Georgetown to Waca Wachee. Rained last night, overcast today. Had some help with the tide at first, then the flooded river (Waccamaw) right in our face, very strong.

Heavy rain last week put the river over its banks. Parking lot at Waca Wachee flooded, but we still love it here!

4/19/03 _____

Headed for Cricket Cove in New River in the morning. Had 2-3 knot current against us till Bucksport. Lots of flooding along the way.

The bridge tender at the new swing bridge at Barefoot Landing appeared to be asleep at the switch. Could not raise him on the radio. After close to an hour, with many vessels backed up in both directions, the bridge opened, with no explanation. We had even been invited to a temp slip to wait for the bridge when it suddenly did open. Go figure!

Remembering how little water there is in the slip area, we opted for one of the two face docks. Shortly after we had docked, a 200 plus foot ACL ship turned up and made to tie up at the other face dock. What ensued was a real Chinese fire drill. One crew member sent over a heaving line to the dockmaster. Before the crew member could send over a mooring line, the dockmaster cleated off the heaving line to the dock and then ran to catch a bow line. Needless to say the ¼ inch heaving line parted in an instant and resulted in much more maneuvering. Lots of fun to watch.

4/20/03 _____

Easter Sunday. Cloudy and cool. Headed for Southport. Sun came out when we arrived at Southport Marina. Went biking, will go shopping in the morning. Only 27 miles to Wrightsville beach tomorrow.

4/21/03 _____

Morning comes sunny and flat. Had a nice run up the Cape Fear River. Passed by Wrightsville Beach in favor of Harbor Village. Very fancy and nice marina. Borrowed courtesy car (truck) and went shopping at a very dirty Food Lion. Yuk!

4/22/03 _____

Left Harbor Village for Swansboro, Dudley's Marina. Cloudy off and on, cold front that had been predicted never came thru. Borrowed courtesy Suburban and food shopped at Lowes Food Store. Nice store, but their computers crashed so it took an hour to check out!

Called Pete and Elaine but their number has been disconnected.

Discovered that the gearbox cooler has been leaking at both ends. Topped off ATF and put a new diaper down. Will check tomorrow

4/23/03 - 4/24/03 _____

Heading for Oriental. Cold front finally came thru, 24 hours late. Cool and breezy.

Found that the Motel is being converted to condo/timeshare. They put in nice new docks.

Met Ed and Betsy Wright onboard HAVEN at the town dock.

Pete and Elaine and Joe and Judy met us for dinner the second night at M&M. We love Oriental!!!

Saw Jim and Doug at the Bean for breakfast. We both got haircuts from Georgie, what a character.

Discovered loose hose connection on the oil cooler. Changed the cooler anyway and made sure all hose connections were tight.

4/25/03 - 4/26/03 _____

Left Oriental for Dowry Creek. Overcast with rain in the late afternoon. This is our first time at Dowry Creek and we loved it. Ed and Betsy were there when we arrived. We had a potluck dinner in the lounge hosted by Donald? and Mary, the marina owners. Beer can chicken. Lots of fun.

Took courtesy van into Belle Haven for shopping. Van pretty old, overheated on the way back. Weather looks gloomy for tomorrow so decided on a layday. Had dinner on HAVEN with Ed and Betsy, fun.

4/27/03 _____

Left Dowry Creek for Alligator River Marina. Cloudy in the morning but cleared in the afternoon. Marina is a hoot! It's really a gas station (for cars) with slips (for boats). Met a boatfull of ladies on ESCAPE.

Their husbands were on a golf vacation, so the girls chartered a 40 foot sailboat for their vacation. Only one of them knew how to sail, but they were having a ball! Had wine and cheese on their boat.

4/28/03 – 4/29/03 _____

On to Elizabeth City. Lovely day. Said goodbye to HAVEN in Albemarle Sound, as they were headed for the Virginia Cut and we were destined for the Dismal Swamp.

The engine overheated just short of Elizabeth City. A machine screw holding the arm that kept tension on the alternator belt let go, so the raw water pump was not pumping. Jury rigged a repair and made it into Pelican Inc. Marina. Walked to a hardware store and bought a HELICOIL for a permanent fix.

Moved to the free City Dock the next day. Had wine and cheese at Fred Fearing's house. What fun. Fred is a great old guy, but a devout racist! That's the way he was brought up.

4/30/03 _____

Left E.C. for the Dismal Swamp Canal. Loved the canal, it really is beautiful. Met some annoying Canadians at the first lock.

Put in to Waterside Marina in Norfolk. This puts you right downtown with lots of restaurants and shopping. Nice.

5/01/03 _____

Left Norfolk for Deltaville. Beautiful day up the bay. Biked to West Marine for some odds and ends. PRINCIPIA still on the ways at Deagles Boatyard. Massive job!

5/02/03 _____

Left Deltaville for Solomons. Day starts out nice, then clouds up, and clearing again late. Took bikes ashore for trip to Food Lion. Nice ride, lilacs in bloom but still early spring.

EIDOLON *at dock in Melbourne, Florida*

5/03/03 _____

Solomons to Annapolis. Cloudy, some rain, the bay was very lumpy. Stayed at Yacht Basin Inc. Got hassled about our length. First time that ever happened. The most unfriendly marina we ever stayed at.

Had dinner ashore, fun. Annapolis much more crowded than the last time.

5/04/03 _____

Headed to Chesapeake City. Stayed at Sheaffer's. This place is really run down now. Some docks caving in. We will not stay there again.

5/06/03 _____

On to Cape May. Cool, gray, some rain. Long day, Delaware Bay was unfriendly. Stayed at Utch's, very nice friendly place. Figured out that this was my 7th stay there. Met up with George (?) on a small sailboat that he is single handing from New Bern to Boothbay. We had seen him earlier at Shaeffer's. Don't envy him his open cockpit on a day like today.

5/07/03 _____

Cape May to Beach Haven, NJ. Morrison's Marina. We opted for the inside route. Morrison's is expensive $2.50/ft and no amenities. Showers were filthy. A real shitty place. Hated the town. Sue fell off her bike and barked up a knee and an elbow. This place didn't do much for my love of New Jersey !

5/08/03 _____

Beach Haven to Manasquan. Lousy day, cold and foggy.

Barnegat Bay is a bad way to go, especially in fog. You cannot see the next day mark until you're right at the previous one. Radar helped a lot. All in all, we hate New Jersey even more than before, if that's possible. Had dinner at the Sand Dollar.

5/09/03 _____

Left Manasquan for Ziegler's cove in Darien. Lumpy in the ocean, gray and cool. Developed problem with the alternator when too many items drawing current, microwave, refer, radar, nav lights. Took refer off-line.

Ziegler's cove was pleasant, sun came out and we had a nice dinner of pork tenderloin.

5/10/03 _____

Left Ziegler's cove in dense fog. Radar was a blessing, could not have made it without.

Got in at 6:30 after a 30-minute wait at the Old Lyme Draw. Met at the dock by Lee, Norm, Kate, Kevin and Sandy. Later by Debbie, David and Amy. Deb brought wine, cheese, paté, crackers, etc. Had a nice party. Left at 9:30 for takeout pizza at Alforno's.

GREAT TO BE HOME!!!

ABOUT THE AUTHOR

Robert (Bob) Higgins started out playing in boats at a very young age. His father, Ted Higgins, built a small rowboat for Bob's older brother Dick and named it WASP for the aircraft carrier of that name. Brother Dick had some fun with it, but wasn't really into boating, so Bob inherited WASP and revelled in it on Holly Pond in Darien, Connecticut. Fitting the boat for sailing, with rickety leeboards, a short mast and rudder, Bob managed to keep from drowning for several summers. Eventually WASP died of old age.

Then followed a series of safer boats including a SUNFISH that Bob built from a kit and a Cape Cod knockabout that needed some major repairs before he began sailing her on Long Island Sound. It was becoming clear that he was destined to spend a lot of time on the water.

Years later Bob earned his 100 ton masters license from the Coast Guard. He held it for twenty years. During that time he served as captain on several charter boats and as one of the captains of the Steamer SABINO at the Mystic Seaport Museum. Additionally, he made numerous passages to and from Bermuda and the Caribbean doing ocean yacht deliveries.

CPSIA information can be obtained
at www.ICGtesting.com
Printed in the USA
LVHW020257190219
607864LV00010B/127/P